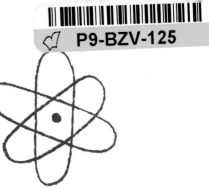

Christiane Dorion • Gosia Herba

INVENTED
by ANIMALS

MEET THE CREATURES WHO INSPIRED
OUR EVERYDAY TECHNOLOGY

WIDE EYED EDITIONS

CONTENTS

To all budding scientists
and inventors of tomorrow – C.D.

To my Beloved Mom, B. – G.H.

 Quarto Knows

Brimming with creative inspiration, how-to projects, and useful information to enrich your everyday life, Quarto Knows is a favourite destination for those pursuing their interests and passions. Visit our site and dig deeper with our books into your area of interest: Quarto Creates, Quarto Cooks, Quarto Homes, Quarto Lives, Quarto Drives, Quarto Explores, Quarto Gifts, or Quarto Kids.

Inspiring | Educating | Creating | Entertaining

Invented by Animals © 2021 Quarto Publishing plc. Text © 2021 Christiane Dorion
Illustrations © 2021 Gosia Herba

First Published in 2021 Wide Eyed Editions, an imprint of The Quarto Group.
400 First Avenue North, Suite 400, Minneapolis, MN 55401, USA.
T (612) 344-8100 F (612) 344-8692 **www.QuartoKnows.com**

A catalogue record for this book is available from the British Library.

ISBN 978-0-7112-6067-2

The illustrations were created digitally
set in Caffeine, Pacifico and Museo

Published by Georgia Amson-Bradshaw
Designed by Myrto Dimitrakoulia
Commissioned and edited by Lucy Brownridge
Production by Dawn Cameron

Manufactured in Guangzhou, China EB 012021

9 8 7 6 5 4 3 2 1

MIX
Paper from
responsible sources
FSC
www.fsc.org FSC® C124385

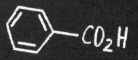

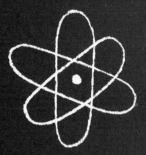

DEAR READER,

Did you know that one of the fastest trains in the world was made quieter and even speedier with the help of the kingfisher? Or that termites helped to design houses that stay cool in hot weather? And that an octopus might hold the recipe for an invisibility cloak?

In this book, you will meet some of the superstar animal inventors who are inspiring humans to develop amazing inventions and solve tricky problems.

When it comes to living in tune with nature, we are the real pros and can certainly teach humans a thing or two! We build smart structures, produce incredible substances, and have shapes that allow us to move smoothly through air, water, and on land. We use materials over and over again without creating any waste. After all, we've survived and thrived on the planet for millions of years so we know what works and what doesn't. No wonder humans often come to us for a helping hand!

Discover some of the brilliant ideas that mimic our tried and tested designs, structures, and superpowers. From sticking to wet surfaces to saving energy, capturing water from the air to running upside down.

You'll never look at bats, dung beetles, jellyfish,
and lots of other animals the same way again.

Yours sincerely,

FROG

... Mimic octopus ...
MASTER OF DISGUISE

I live in tropical seas and spend much of my time in shallow sandy waters where there are very few places to hide. As you can see, I don't have a shell or sharp spines to defend myself. When I swim in the open sea looking for food, my soft, boneless body makes me a tasty morsel for sharks, barracudas, and other hungry creatures.

So, how do I survive...?

the Octopus Stories

... I am a master of disguise! I can quickly change the color of my skin to scare away predators or to blend in with my surroundings. I can wriggle or even hide some of my eight spindly arms to copy the shapes and movements of more threatening animals and warn my enemies to keep clear. The disguises I use depend on what I think my audience will find most scary.

Sometimes I glide along the seabed, playing the part of a poisonous flatfish, tucking my arms back into a flat shape. I can also propel myself through the water with my arms out to look like lionfish spines. I am a versatile actor! Damselfish are particular enemies of mine but I know they are scared of being eaten by sea snakes. If I see a damselfish, I hide under the sand pretending to be a sea snake with just two stripy arms on show.

I have perfected my mimic art over millions of years. Tiny sensors all over my skin quickly survey my surroundings and tell my body when to turn on the right disguise. Humans are looking into my nifty technique to try to make a material that will instantly camouflage to its surroundings. **With my help, you might one day have your very own invisibility cloak!**

… Blue morpho butterfly …
COLOR WITH STRUCTURE

I am simply radiant in the spotlight!
I was born to shine. When the light hits me,
I am transformed from a dull creature to
a gleaming blue beauty. But it is all a show,
an illusion, as my wings are not actually blue!

My stage is the Amazon rainforest,
and I am one of the biggest butterflies
on the planet. My bright wings make
me stand out in the dark jungle, but
also send the signal "Don't dare to
eat me!" What makes me special is
the way my wings manipulate light to
create this striking blue.

Nature is full of vibrant colors, from the bright yellows and greens
of noisy parrots to the pinks and purples of delicate flowers. Most
colors are created by substances called pigments. In my case, the
gorgeous blue I wear comes from rows and rows of microscopic
scales that cover the top of my wings. These scales act like tiny
prisms, reflecting and scattering light in such a way that makes my
wings appear a vibrant blue. It is all a clever trick of the light.

With my light-powered technique, I can help humans add color to textiles without using chemicals that can harm the environment. My dazzling technology could also be used to make special banknotes that are impossible to forge or give anything a color that looks fabulous in the light.

· THE PRISM ·

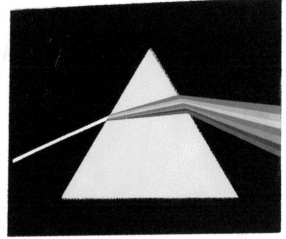

Light travels as a wave, a bit like a ripple on a pond, but the waves are so tiny that we can't see them. White light is made of different colors. When it enters a prism, it bends and splits into distinct colors, like those of a rainbow.

··· Shark ···
SLEEK SWIMMER

Known for my hunting prowess, I have a muscular body and sharp teeth but I'm also super fast. My ancestors were patrolling the seas around 450 million years ago, well before dinosaurs. It's fair to say I've swum around the block a few times and my body has adapted in amazing ways to help me do it fast. No wonder humans come to me when they need underwater speed.

Want to know my secret? It's skin deep! My skin may look as soft as silk, but it is as rough as sandpaper. I am covered in tiny scales with little grooves and channels that help water flow along my body and reduce drag, allowing me to swim faster. The rough surface of my skin also stops barnacles, seaweed, and other clingy things from hitching a ride, which would, of course, slow me down.

My special skin has already inspired clever inventions. It has been mimicked to create high-tech swimsuits, which made a real splash at the 2000 Olympics. Alas, these were later banned in international sports events, due to too many world records being broken by super-fast swimmers using them.

I have also inspired the invention of a special coating for ships and submarines that mimics the rough surface of my skin and stops barnacles from sticking to them. It means humans don't have to use toxic paint that pollutes the sea and harms marine life.

I've got so many projects I want to turn my fin to. A "shark skin" super material could increase the efficiency of machines, from planes and drones to wind turbines. And it would save energy too! My skin technology could also help to stop germs sticking to surfaces in busy places like hospitals, buses, and trains.

Before long, shark-skin tech could be everywhere and my bad reputation, a thing of the past!

MASTER BUILDERS

We are some of the very best builders in the animal world. See how we use materials and shapes in ingenious ways to build awe-inspiring structures. All made with local resources and without a shred of waste!

LODGE

POND

DAM

UNDERWATER ENTRANCE

Beaver
FLOOD DEFENCES

My teeth are my tool kit. I cut down trees with them and build dams across rivers and streams, using branches, mud, and weeds. A dam slows the flow of a river and creates a pond of still water where I can make a safe, dry lodge for my family.

As climate change brings about more extreme weather, humans can learn a few tips from us on how to control flooding.

Termite
AIR-CONDITIONED HOME

We may be small but we build big. The huge mounds we construct are made just with soil, spit, and dung. We live in hot savannas, and without electricity we had to think up our own air-con system. We build tunnels, chimneys and vents that allow hot, stale air to rise up and escape, and cooler air to sink down.

Inspired by our mounds, humans now design buildings that cool themselves. Thanks to us you can say goodbye to energy-guzzling air conditioning.

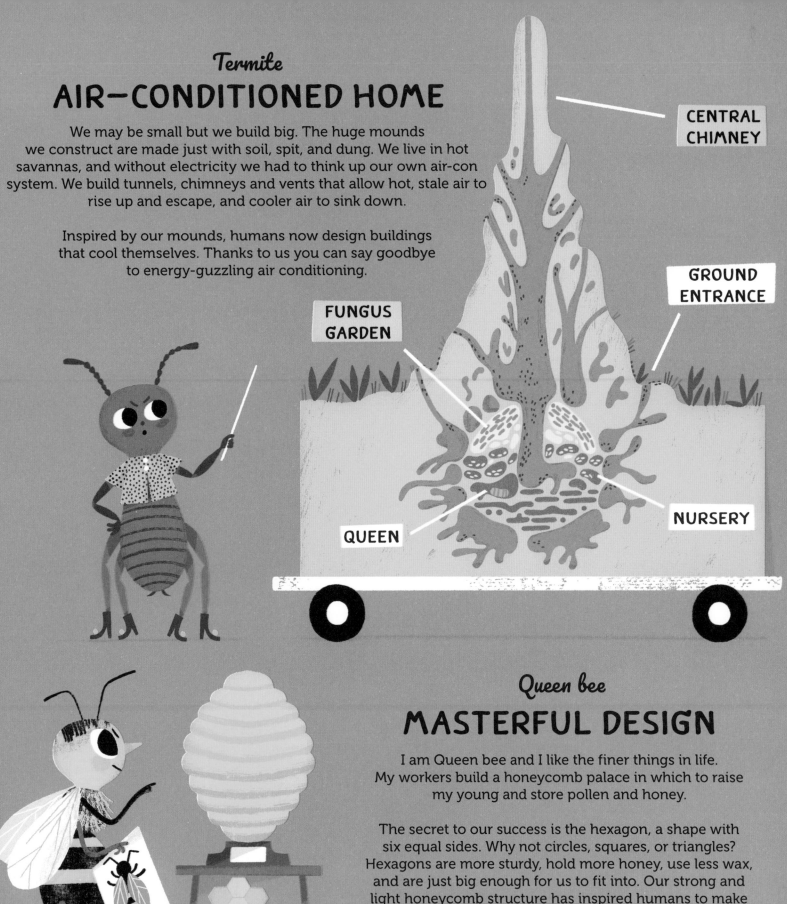

CENTRAL CHIMNEY

GROUND ENTRANCE

FUNGUS GARDEN

NURSERY

QUEEN

Queen bee
MASTERFUL DESIGN

I am Queen bee and I like the finer things in life. My workers build a honeycomb palace in which to raise my young and store pollen and honey.

The secret to our success is the hexagon, a shape with six equal sides. Why not circles, squares, or triangles? Hexagons are more sturdy, hold more honey, use less wax, and are just big enough for us to fit into. Our strong and light honeycomb structure has inspired humans to make many things, from cardboard packaging to shoe soles, automobile wheels, bridges, and even airplanes.

··· Eagle ···
SUPER-ZOOM VISION

I am one of the largest and most powerful birds of prey on the planet, often praised for my formidable hunting skills. With my sharp talons, I can snatch a slippery fish out of water or grab a rabbit off the ground while in full flight and, with my curved beak, I can rend it apart. But what am I most proud of? My eyes. Sharing my vision with the world is inspiring amazing photography! I will tell you how.

E
F P
T O Z
P D L E
D E F Z C
F C Z D E P
L E P Z D F O
F P O T E F O L

Due to the unique structure of my eyes, I can zoom in like a telescope lens and spot ripples on a lake or small movements on the ground while soaring in the sky. I then swoop down at up to 99 miles per hour, keeping my prey in sharp focus throughout my descent.

EAGLE EYE

HUMAN EYE

If humans had eyes like mine, they would be able to see an ant crawling on the ground from the roof of a ten-story building. My vision is not only sharper than yours but I can also see colors more vividly. Having eyes wide apart gives me a broader field of vision, extending nearly all the way around my head.

Humans have used my eye technology to build a miniature camera, as small as the tip of a pen. Powerful lenses this small could help them develop micro-robots to look inside the human body and many other micro-machines that can zoom in on details just like me.

··· Gecko ···
RUNNING UPSIDE DOWN

I live in warm climates and like to hang around in people's houses. Humans don't mind me, as I gobble up cockroaches, locusts, mosquitoes, and other unwelcome guests. Gymnastically gifted, I can run up walls and along ceilings without falling off and even hang from glass on just a single toe! But guess what? My feet aren't sticky at all!

My plump toes are covered in thousands of microscopic hairs, each one of these split into hundreds of finer ends. These are so tiny that they can grip the molecules of the surface I am walking on and enable me to cling to it. I can also turn the stickiness of my feet on and off. To loosen my grip, I just need to peel my toes away before raising my foot. Impressive, isn't it?

Running upside down is only one of my party tricks. I can also lick my lidless eyeballs with my tongue to keep them clean and shed my tail for a quick escape. Don't worry, I can grow a new one!

I've shared the secret of my grippy feet with humans and, by copying my toe hairs, they have invented a strong tape that can be peeled and used repeatedly. Imagine all the things that could be stuck together with gecko tape, without using heat or stuff that pollutes nature. **Perhaps one day humans will be able to climb up smooth, shiny skyscrapers wearing gecko shoes.**

··· Seahorse ···
A TERRIFIC TAIL

I may not look like one, but **I am a fish.** I have fins, a swim bladder, and I breathe through gills. I'm tiny and the slowest swimmer in the sea, so you might be wondering what I have to offer to the world of inventions. Well, small is mighty and I'm an all-natural piece of design perfection. Let me tell you about my terrific tail.

My tail is rock hard, yet delicate and flexible! I use it to anchor myself to grasses and coral, even in strong currents. At times, I also hold tails with my mate so we can float together, side by side, for hours. It's practical AND romantic.

Humans have always found me adorable, but they are now intrigued by the unique geometry of my tail. While lizards, monkeys, and most other animals have round tails, mine is square! Oddly enough, this makes me much better at grasping things while able to bend and twist.

Unlike other fish I don't have scales. My body is protected by square bony plates all the way down to my curly tail, like a strong suit of armor. These plates slide over each other, allowing my tail to twist, bend, or even be crushed and quickly return to its original shape.

Using my tail technology, scientists are working out how to make lightweight body protection and robots that are strong and flexible enough to be able to grip things.

Who would have thought that a small, peculiar fish like me, the horse of the sea, could teach humans how to invent better, stronger machines!

··· Paper wasp ···
EXPERT PAPER MAKER

I can be a real nuisance as I buzz around and raid summer picnics in search of sugary treats. I have a fearsome sting but, may I say, only use it to defend myself when provoked. But did you know that I'm also a master paper maker?

MILK

NEST

SUGARY TREATS
WASP
paper CRAFTS

ARCHITECTURE

Picnic Raid
· PAPER
· COLLAGE

ORIGAMI
A WASP'S LIFE

PAPER

PAPIER-MÂCHÉ
Sting

Paper wasps like me invented paper long before humans. We gather bits of wood and chew them into a soft pulp, which we use to construct our nest. As the pulp dries, it hardens and makes a cosy, waterproof home in which our queen can lay her eggs. Even though our papery nest is super strong, it breaks down naturally over the winter and we build a new one the following spring.

Humans have been making paper since ancient times with plants and old rags. Around 105 AD a Chinese man called Cai Lun, who worked for the emperor, came up with the idea of turning wood into pulp by watching us make our nests. Hundreds of years later, mighty machines were invented to cut down forests and turn trees into pulp for paper.

CAI LUN

COOKIE

ART of PAPER

ORIGAMI

SKETCHBOOK

ink

ink

Thank goodness humans have now figured out how to recycle paper. Of course, recycling is also something that we and all other animals have been doing for millions of years!

⋯ Tree frog ⋯
A FORMIDABLE GRIP

As a tree frog, I spend most of my time in trees near rivers, streams, and ponds where it is damp and wet. Lots of animals want to eat me so it is important I don't slip when crawling up tree bark or hopping from leaf to leaf. What's the gripping secret that stops me falling off slippery surfaces, even on rainy days?

CROAK
CROAK

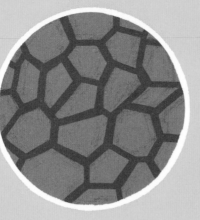

It's all about the unique design of my toe pads. If you looked at them under a microscope, you would see a pattern of tiny grooves shaped like hexagons. When my feet touch a wet surface, the grooves produce a watery goo, helping me to cling on. Bits of trapped dirt are pushed to the tips of my pads while I move, always keeping my feet nice and clean.

GLUE glue

FROG ROBOT

My toe-tally unique gripping pattern is inspiring many cool ideas, from automobile tires that stick better to wet and icy roads, to a self-cleaning sticky tape that can be used again and again without losing its grip.

FROGS: jumping

Humans have also built a small medical robot that uses my gripping technology to move inside the slippery human body and could one day help surgeons to perform difficult operations.

··· Earwig ···
ORIGAMI WINGS

I am an ordinary kind of bug found all over the world. I'm not an attention seeker. I don't have the bright colors of a butterfly or the shiny spots of a ladybug. My menacing pincers make me look much scarier than I am. But I do have one big secret...

... I have huge hidden wings intricately folded and tucked away. They can expand to ten times their size and stay open without any muscle power. With just one click, they quickly retract so I can squeeze back into the tight, dark places where I live. I rarely fly, but my wings come in handy for a quick escape.

Humans are very intrigued by my wings. The way they unfurl and refold into such a tiny space even defy the rules of origami, the art of paper folding. Astronauts are looking at how my folded wings could help to design better space probes, robots, and solar sails that power satellites. These all need to fit inside a rocket and unfold once in space so could do with a bit of earwig origami power!

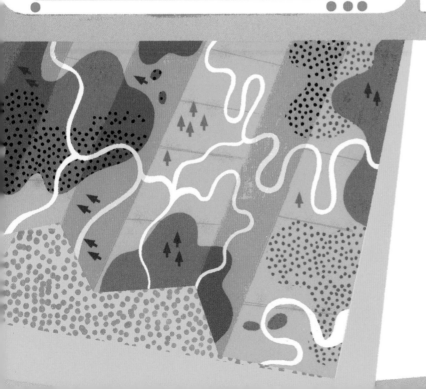

Solving the mystery of my wings could help humans to create better designs for lots of other things that need to be folded into compact shapes, like tents, packaging, and even electronic gadgets. Can you think of any others?

So next time you go on a bug hunt, think about my extraordinary wings packed neatly away.

···Jumbo squid···
SELF-REPAIRING TEETH

I like to keep myself to myself and humans don't know much about me, as I live in the deep dark ocean. For centuries I have been talked about in stories as a giant sea monster, dragging ships into the depths with my long tentacles. But I'm no monster and have a lot to teach humans. I have enormous eyes, two long feeding tentacles, three hearts, and eight giant arms. I can change color in the blink of an eye and squirt out dark clouds of ink to confuse my enemies.

But that's not all! I have lines of suckers on my arms and tentacles, each one ringed with sharp teeth, which I use to latch on to my prey. Not only are they super strong but my teeth also repair themselves if damaged. No fillings or trips to the dentist for me!

Inspired by my smart, self-repairing teeth, humans have managed to create in their labs a tough material that can mend itself with water. In the future, you might be able to fix your torn football shirt or a smashed phone screen with just a little water, thanks to me.

I'm also an eco-warrior. Easily repairable objects mean less waste and a happier planet. This so-called monster is here to help humans clean up their act! **What else do you think my special powers could be used for?**

··· Spider ···
WEB DESIGNER

Lots of people think I am scary, although I am not quite sure why. After all, I am just a simple arachnid with eight hairy legs, four pairs of beady eyes, and two small venomous fangs. I am quite shy and tend to hide away. You are likely to see my web rather than me and I like it that way.

I have a cunning way to catch my dinner. I spin a large web out of strong, sticky silk, which I make with special glands in my body. When a flying bug gets stuck in my web, I feel the vibrations through the hairs on my legs and rush into action. I stun my victim with a venomous bite, wrap it in sticky silk and stash it for later.

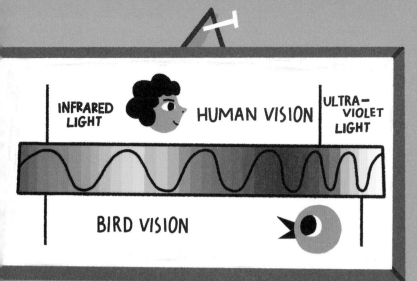

INFRARED LIGHT

HUMAN VISION

ULTRA-VIOLET LIGHT

BIRD VISION

Humans came to me with a special problem only a pro web designer could solve. Large windows of tall buildings are a real danger to birds, as they get confused by the reflection of the sky, and fly into them. To stop birds from colliding with my web, I add special silk threads that reflect ultraviolet light from the sun. Birds can see it but humans can't. My secret trick has inspired the invention of a new bird-friendly glass with a criss-cross pattern that is visible to birds, but not to humans.

My silk is also famous for its superpowers, stretchy and light, yet tougher than steel. Imagine all the things humans will be able to make when they figure out how to replicate it. And it's eco-friendly too!

So, as you can see, we spiders are nothing to fear. We are true environmentalists. We help save birds even though they like to eat us for dinner.

THE ART OF FLYING

Ever noticed how all airplanes look a bit like birds? No coincidence, we pretty much invented flying. When humans wanted to learn how to fly, they tried to copy us. They got it wrong for centuries, even strapping large feather wings to their arms and building bizarre flapping machines. Of course they didn't work. But the principles of flying are actually quite simple. We can fly because of our streamlined bodies and the shapes of our wings. When humans finally worked this out, they made a bird-shaped contraption called an airplane!

GLIDING

I'm an albatross and I fly long haul. Travel is exhausting, so I save my energy by gliding. I spread my long, narrow wings out to catch rising swells of warm air called thermals. A glider plane has no engine at all and wings modeled on mine. No motor power needed!

SOARING

"Soaring like an eagle" is sort of my signature. Some planes copy my curled wing tips to help reduce drag, which is good for soaring up, up, and up.

LIFT

Air moves faster over the top of our curved wings than below. So there is less air pressure above our wings and more underneath. The pressure underneath pushes up and this is called lift. Wings on a plane work in the same way.

AIR

AIR

"V" FORMATION

Birds of a feather FLY together and we geese fly in a "V" formation to conserve energy, taking turns to lead. The leader creates little swirls of air with its wings, making it easier for the other birds behind. Fighter jets do this too so that they use up less fuel.

We still have lots to offer to help humans make better planes and other flying machines, so they can migrate further and faster, but also use less fuel and help to keep our planet clean.

35

··· Namib beetle ···
FOG CATCHER

I am a lonesome long-legged beetle living in one of the driest places on the planet, the African Namib Desert. With very little rain, plants and animals need to be resourceful to survive here. I might be the size of a blueberry but I am pretty smart at finding water. I hear that people like to sunbathe, well I love to... fog-bathe!

Early in the morning, a light fog drifts over the desert from the ocean. I climb to the top of a dune, face into the wind, and stick my bottom up into the air to trap the fog. My back is covered in tiny bumps and grooves. Small droplets of water collect on the bumps and build up before running down the grooves into my mouth.

NamibDesert.

FOG CATCHING

Inspired by my fog-basking technique and bumpy back, humans have created a material that can extract water droplets from the air. With this, they could make nets and other devices able to harvest water from fog in places where there is very little rain. No energy required!

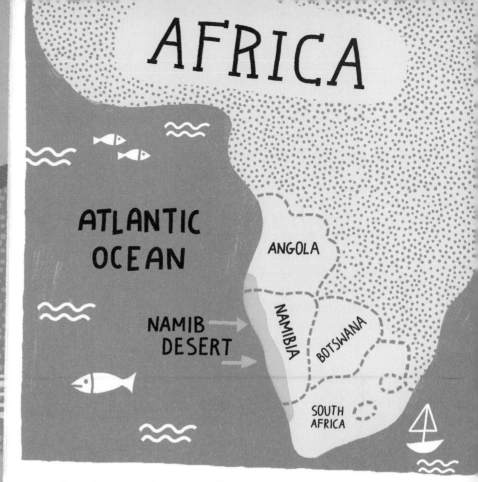

ATLANTIC OCEAN

AFRICA

ANGOLA

NAMIBIA

BOTSWANA

NAMIB DESERT

SOUTH AFRICA

One day you might even have a smart water bottle that can refill itself by drawing moisture from the air, as I do. Very handy for outdoor adventures and camping trips!

Pulling water from the air by standing on my head is not a bad trick for a small desert beetle! It could change the world.

··· Humpback whale ···
BUMPY FLIPPERS

Despite being the size of a bus, I can turn and twirl as gracefully as a nippy little fish. I can jump into the air and perform acrobatic tumbles before diving back into the water with a big splash. I can also swim upwards in small circles, to herd large shoals of krill and fish into a nice ball and eventually into my giant mouth. A tasty trick! The secret to my surprising agility is all in the flipper.

Us whales have been around for a while, so we've had plenty of time to become super efficient in the water. Look closely at my flippers and you can see the row of bumps along the front edge. These change the way water flows, reducing drag and helping me to make tight turns.

At first, humans were puzzled by my knobbly flippers. They studied them carefully and discovered that bumpy blades can be more efficient than smooth ones, both in the water and in the air. So they added a bumpy edge to the blades of wind turbines to capture more energy from the wind. Not only do these work better, but they are much quieter and less likely to stop turning in light winds.

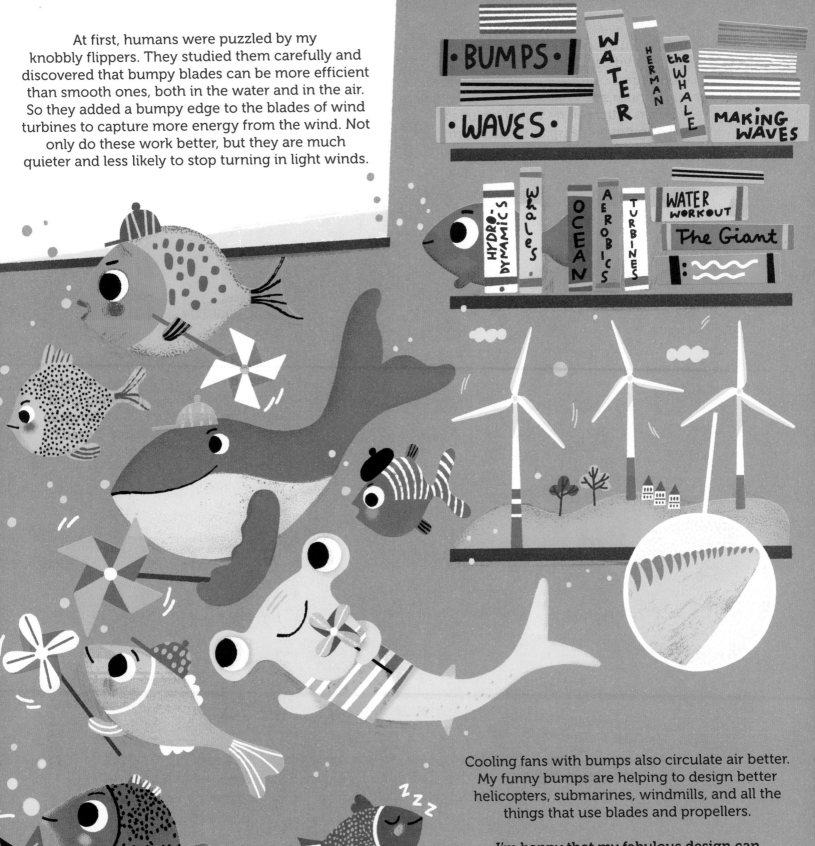

Cooling fans with bumps also circulate air better. My funny bumps are helping to design better helicopters, submarines, windmills, and all the things that use blades and propellers.

I'm happy that my fabulous design can help humans to protect the planet and make even more wind power than ever.

··· Penguin ···
WATERPROOF COAT

Sure, I can't fly or walk very gracefully but I am pretty good at swimming and keeping warm. This comes in handy as I spend a lot of time in very cold water looking for food for my family.

Imagine taking a bath of icy water in freezing weather. Welcome to my world! I am an emperor penguin and live in the coldest place on Earth, Antarctica. I look quite dapper in my black-and-white suit but it's more than just a snappy look. It's the best waterproof coat nature has to offer. Even when I'm swimming under the ice pack, my feathers keep me warm and completely dry.

It's all down to the smart design of my plumage. The small oily feathers that cover my body are super compact and waterproof. They overlap to keep the layer of soft, fluffy down feathers underneath dry, so I can stay warm. Mimicking my waterproof coat could help to develop the ultimate fabric to keep you warm and dry in the cold and wet, just like me.

Here is another cool trick.
I can launch myself out of the sea and land safely on the ice. I do this by releasing tiny bubbles of air trapped in my feathers, which enable me to rocket up to the surface and leap out of the water. Using the same technique by releasing bubbles along the bottom of ships could help reduce friction and save fuel. **I might be a flightless bird but I'm certainly a world champion at bubble surfing!**

··· Polar bear ···
SUNTRAP FUR COAT

Don't be fooled by my cuddly looks! I am a big and powerful bear, built to survive in the harsh, freezing Arctic. Most of the time, I roam on the sea ice or wait patiently by a hole for a plump seal to pop up for air. A blizzard is just normal everyday weather for me!

I'M <u>NOT</u> COOL WITH GLOBAL WARMING!

BEARS

GUARD HAIR

UNDERFUR

SKIN

LAYER OF FAT

Thanks to my special fur and a thick layer of fat, I can stay warm and cosy. But there is a lot more to my fur than meets the eye. You may think I'm white, but I'm not! The long outer hairs of my fur are clear and hollow, like tiny straws, scattering light and making me appear white. They help to trap heat. But that's not all! Underneath my plush fur coat, my skin is actually black, which also helps to soak up the sun's heat and keep me warm.

My ultimate insulation is inspiring humans to develop better materials to capture and absorb the sun's heat. In the future, you could well live in homes kept warm by polar bear solar technology and wear warmer winter clothes, all thanks to me!

Because of human activity, the planet is warming up and the sea ice I depend on is melting. New inventions using solar power will certainly help to save my home. **But every little action helps, too.**

··· Kingfisher ···
DIVING WITHOUT A SPLASH

Humans came to me with a noisy problem. The super speedy bullet train they had built was far too loud. Every time the train blasted out of a tunnel at high speed, it made an explosive BOOM that could be heard for miles around. A cushion of air was building up in front of the train in the tunnel and expanding with a loud bang coming out of it. Passengers and people living along the route were not at all happy with this! But thanks to me, the bullet train was saved.

The unique shape of my beak helped to fix the problem. To catch food, I dive head first into water and quickly return to my perch, hopefully with a fish snack in my beak. My long pointed bill is perfectly shaped for plunging into water at top speed without making a splash so that I don't scare away the fish. The water flows past my beak rather than being pushed in front of it.

Inspired by my splashless dive, the front of the bullet train was redesigned to mimic my long, pointy beak. The new train is much quieter, even faster, and uses less energy. No more BOOM!

OLD DESIGN

TUNNEL → EXIT

AIR BUILDING UP

TUNNEL → EXIT

MASSIVE BOOM

Another problem was the loud whistling sound made by the power cable connector on the roof of the train. The clever old owl inspired a new, quieter design. It was just a matter of copying the shape of its saw-toothed feathers, which break the air and help it to hunt silently.

And that is how one of the world's most high-tech trains was rescued by two wise old birds, the kingfisher and the owl.

45

··· Dragonfly ···
CONTROLLED FLIGHT

I stand out from the bug crowd with my long, slender body, enormous eyes, bright colors, and see-through wings that shimmer in the sun. My ancestors were flitting in the sky over 300 million years ago, long before dinosaurs and birds arrived on the scene! So we've had plenty of time to perfect and hone our flying skills.

Besides my good looks, I am one of the fastest flying bugs in the entire world. My four wings move independently so I can hover, fly up and down, forwards and backwards, and even upside down. I can also speed up really fast and change direction in a split second. This makes me the perfect sky hunter, able to catch a mosquito mid-flight with amazing speed and control.

My flight ability has inspired the invention of a small four-winged drone that flies just like me. It's swift, agile, and can hold its position even in strong gusts of wind. Rigged with a tiny camera, it could be used for search-and-rescue missions in places that are difficult to access.

DRAGONFLY

DRONE

Maybe my large bubble eyes could also inspire cool inventions? Made of thousands of little lenses, they enable me to see almost everywhere at once, so it's hard to sneak up on me.

Oh and one more thing. Don't worry if I land on your head, I don't bite and it's a sign of good luck!

··· Woodpecker ···
LEAD DRUMMER

I'm quite hard to spot but you might have heard my rapid tap-tap-tap when walking in the woods. Unlike other birds, I am more of a drummer than a singer and a real head banger. Knocking my head against a tree trunk is what I do best! I can drum up to 22 times per second to call a mate or to let other birds know that this is my patch of woodland. I also peck on tree bark to find bugs or chisel out a nest.

NECK MUSCLES

SPONGY BONE

BEAK

HORSESHOE-SHAPED BONE

I may look fragile but my body is built for head banging. My long, pointed beak is flexible on the outside but sturdy on the inside. As well as a thick skull, I have two special bones that act as shock absorbers. One is spongy like a cushion, the other holds my brain like a safety belt. And my strong neck muscles are the envy of any serious body builder.

My clever design is being copied to try to make safer helmets for footballers, cyclists, motor racers or anyone else who needs a helmet. It could be used for other things that need to resist knocks and shocks like automobile bumpers, flight recorders for planes, spacecraft, and much more.

Why bang your head against a brick wall when the solution for safe shock absorbing has already been found by the most successful head-banging wood-pecking bird?

··· Snake ···

SLITHERING CHAMPION

Us snakes live everywhere, from scorching deserts to steamy jungles. Ssslithering is our ssspeciality! With our long, bendy bodies, we can slither and slide smoothly over boulders, fallen trees, or sandy slopes. We can climb up trees, squeeze into tight spaces, and even dart through water. This is when we're not too busy sunbathing on a rock to warm up.

We don't have legs so we use our muscles and scales to push ourselves along the ground in our unique, slithery way. We also have a long flexible spine and hundreds of small bones connected together to allow us to bend and curl. Some of us wiggle from side to side, others bunch up and straighten like an accordion. Some move sideways, others creep forwards in a straight line.

ACCORDION

STRAIGHT

Humans are studying how we move to create the ultimate snake robots. They have designed robots of all sizes, with lots of different segments that work together, just like a snake's body. Long, thin robots could help to find survivors under earthquake rubble or explore the ancient pyramids of Egypt. Micro-size ones might even be able to wiggle inside the human body to help doctors and surgeons.

Some day, snake robots could be slithering everywhere, navigating treacherous terrain, climbing obstacles, or squeezing into tiny holes. They might even be rocketed to Mars to explore its bumpy surface without tipping over or getting stuck.

Adding small cameras or heat sensors, like those we use to detect our prey in the dark, could make these robots even smarter!

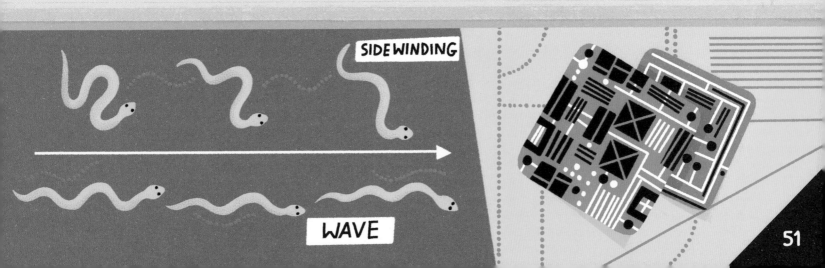

SIDEWINDING

WAVE

··· Jellyfish ···
LOW-ENERGY SWIMMING

I look a bit like an alien with my see-through squishy body and dangling tentacles. I'm mostly made of water and have no heart, no bones, and no brain. Yet jellies like me have been around for over 500 million years! And it would be hard to match our efficiency when it comes to pulsing along in the sea.

I don't swim fast like a fish and mostly drift with the tides and currents. But I have a knack for propelling myself forward using very little energy. I open my bell-shaped body to suck water in and squeeze it to force the water out, pushing me gently along. It's very slow but effortless.

Jelly!

Soft, squishy robots pumping their way slowly through the ocean might be the future of underwater machines. With climate change, oil spills, and plastic pollution, our home is seriously threatened. So humans are trying to build jelly-like robots that could glide silently through the water to explore coral reefs and the deep ocean, collect useful information, and help protect all the creatures that live in the sea.

Like us, these robots might have to watch out for peckish sea turtles that could mistake them for their favorite snack!

··· Locust ···
AVOIDING COLLISION

We locusts are a kind of grasshopper found in hot, arid parts of the world and usually settle for a quiet, solitary life. Our drab brown color helps us to blend in and we don't like to mingle.

But when rain comes, everything changes. Young hoppers hatch quickly in their thousands. They are bright yellow, have a huge appetite, and are soon all over the place. We all join together in an enormous frenzied swarm. A dense cloud of millions of us can darken the sky and devour all the plants and food crops growing in our path, leaving humans with very little to eat.

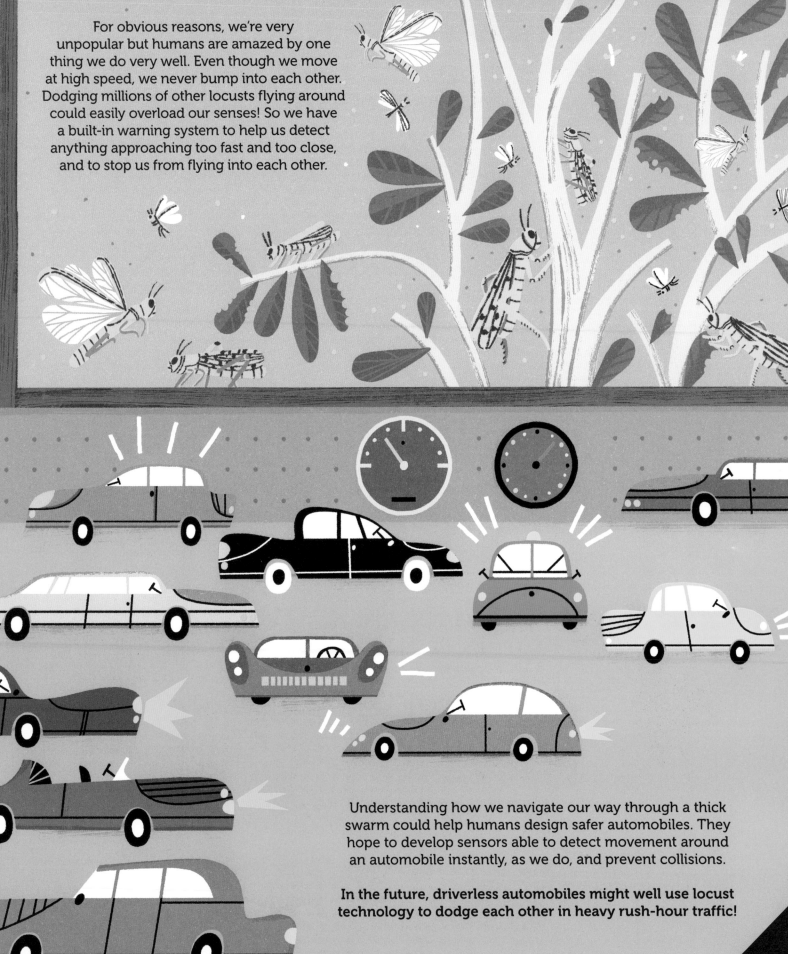

For obvious reasons, we're very unpopular but humans are amazed by one thing we do very well. Even though we move at high speed, we never bump into each other. Dodging millions of other locusts flying around could easily overload our senses! So we have a built-in warning system to help us detect anything approaching too fast and too close, and to stop us from flying into each other.

Understanding how we navigate our way through a thick swarm could help humans design safer automobiles. They hope to develop sensors able to detect movement around an automobile instantly, as we do, and prevent collisions.

In the future, driverless automobiles might well use locust technology to dodge each other in heavy rush-hour traffic!

ROBOT WORLD

Robots are amazing, and many of them are inspired by animals. They copy the way we fly, swim, run, climb, hop, or scuttle quickly through obstacles. Some are designed to do dangerous jobs like searching through rubble left by tornadoes or earthquakes. Others can squeeze into tiny places where humans can't fit. Some are built to explore deep-sea trenches or even faraway planets. Others are just cool or fun! If you had to design your own robot, which animal would be your inspiration?

Etruscan shrew
NIGHTTIME NAVIGATOR

I might be the smallest mammal in the world but when it comes to hunting in total darkness, I'm a real pro, thanks to my touchy feely whiskers. This cute robot moves its whiskers back and forth like I do to sense objects and feel its way around in dark places.

Bee
BUZZING AROUND

Meet the world's smallest winged robot, inspired by me. One day, colonies of these tiny robo-critters could give us a hand with pollinating flowers and food crops.

Cockroach
GETTING OUT OF TIGHT SPACES

My tank-like build, super-fast scuttle speed, and ability to flatten my body to squeeze through small gaps have inspired this small robot. If it gets squished, it compresses itself and keeps scurrying along, just like me!

HEIGHT
75mm

HEIGHT
35mm

Manta ray
UNDERWATER ROBOTS

So many secrets and treasures are yet to be discovered in the ocean depths!
Robots disguised as fish like me could help humans explore and protect
our seas without disturbing the creatures that live here.

··· Shipworm ···
TUNNELING

My long, soft body makes me look like a worm but I'm actually a mollusk, just like a clam or a mussel. I am notoriously known for boring into wood submerged in seawater. In the old days, when ships were only made of wood, shipworms like me could chew their hulls to pieces. Nowadays we mainly munch on piers, jetties and old shipwrecks.

ARCHITECTURE

TWO SIPHONS

SHELLS

MOUTH

GUT FULL OF WOOD DUST

WATER IN

WATER OUT

You may think boring sounds boring, but not the way I do it. I use the little jagged shells that protect my soft head to bore into wood. As I slowly eat the wood, I produce a substance that lines and reinforces the tunnel behind me. It's pretty smart and keeps me safe.

·THAMES TUNNEL·

MARC BRUNEL

HOW TO MAKE A TUNNEL

LEXICON OF TUNNELS

Ships

WOOD

The famous engineer Marc Brunel was a real fan of my way of tunneling. He built the world's first underwater tunnel under the River Thames in London in the early 19th century. Brunel noticed my unusual technique on an old piece of timber riddled with holes. Inspired by the shells on my head, he invented the tunneling shield to protect diggers from falling earth. He also took the idea of lining the tunnel with layers of bricks as they dug to stop the walls from collapsing.

Thanks to Brunel, I might now be remembered as a smart tunnel engineer rather than a ship-sinking mollusk.

··· Dolphin ···
SECRET LANGUAGE

I live in the ocean and love surfing on waves, blowing bubbles, and leaping out of the water with a splash. I'm very sociable and can be a real chatterbox when swimming with my pod. We whistle and squeak, and make all sorts of sounds to talk to one another. We also shake our heads, clap our jaws, and even slap the water with our flippers and tails. Each one of us has a signature whistle so we know who's talking.

LOW
FREQUENCY
HIGH

ECHOLOCATION

SENDING

RECEIVING

We use high-pitched clicks to sense our surroundings and find food. These produce sound waves that travel far and fast through the water. When they hit something like a rock or a fish, they bounce back as echoes, even in dark or murky water. From this, we can work out the size and shape of the object and how far away it is. It's like seeing with sound!

Humans also use sound waves to navigate, detect objects, or communicate underwater. In the past they have found it tricky to stop their messages being disrupted by the sound of crashing waves or other underwater noises. That's where we come in! We constantly change the pitch of our calls to cut through all the other sounds. **Now humans have learned our secret, they are sending clearer messages than ever before.**

··· Bat ···
SONAR

ECHOLOCATION

What does a bat like me, with beady little eyes and razor-sharp teeth, have in common with a smiley dolphin? Surprisingly, we're both mammals and we both rely on sound to navigate and hunt in the dark.

Being nocturnal, I spend my day hanging upside down in caves, tree hollows, and old buildings, and only come out to hunt after dark. I make high-pitched chirping sounds that bounce back to my ears when they hit an object, a bit like a boomerang. This is how I find my way around and catch tasty flying bugs, with incredible precision.

Inspired by how animals like us can detect our surroundings through sounds and echoes, humans invented radar to track objects like planes and ships. Now they are turning to us again to help their robots navigate in the dark, smoke, or bad weather without cameras.

I'm also the only mammal in the world that can fly and I'm remarkably good at it. My stretchy bat wings might help to develop nimble robots that can swoop and dive like I do. **Even robots can learn from old tricks!**

MIGHTY RECYCLERS

We were busy recycling long before humans worked out that waste can be turned into treasure. In the natural world, nothing goes to waste. We take only what we need and recycle everything, over and over again. Meet some of our top recyclers who are doing their bit to keep the planet clean.

Bird
LOCAL MATERIALS

We build our nests with whatever we can get our claws on to make them warm, safe, and cosy for our chicks. We use twigs, dead leaves, sticky cobwebs, fur, or feathers. Sometimes, we even add bits of string, paper, or plastic bags left behind by humans.

Dung beetle
A BIG BALL OF POOP

We take recycling to another level. Poop is our world! We roll it into a ball so we can wheel it easily to a good spot. We then bury it in the ground to munch on later and lay our eggs in it. And we don't make a stink about it!

Hermit crab
SECONDHAND HOMES

We don't grow our own shells so, to protect ourselves, we borrow old ones abandoned by sea snails and other creatures. When we outgrow a shell, we move into a bigger one. So we constantly reuse other creatures' old dwellings.

Earthworm
EXPERT GARDENER

We are nature's clean-up crew! We feed on dead plants and animals and turn them into rich soil. As we burrow through the ground, we also plough the soil and let air and water in, helping new plants to grow. Without us, waste would just pile up.

Perhaps humans could follow our lead by taking only what they need from nature and making things in a way that means materials can be used again and again, forever. We all have to make sure that we keep our planet clean.

··· Porcupine ···
PRICKLY QUILLS

I live life at a slow pace and am usually out and about after dark. When not up a tree, I shuffle and waddle along, munching on bark, leaves, and twigs with my large front teeth.

I might be slow but watch out! My wild hairdo is actually made from thousands of long sharp quills, which I use to warn off wolves, bears, and other predators. When threatened, I raise my quills to make me look bigger. I rattle them, grunt, and stomp my feet as a warning. If that doesn't work, I turn around and charge backwards to drive quills into my attacker.

So what have my quills inspired?
They can pierce skin easily but are very hard to pull out.
This is because they have tiny hook-like barbs on their tips
that splay out when you try to remove them. Humans are
looking at how staples used to close wounds after surgery
could be designed like my quills. These could leave less
room for infection, speed up healing, and dissolve
naturally so no need to pull them out.

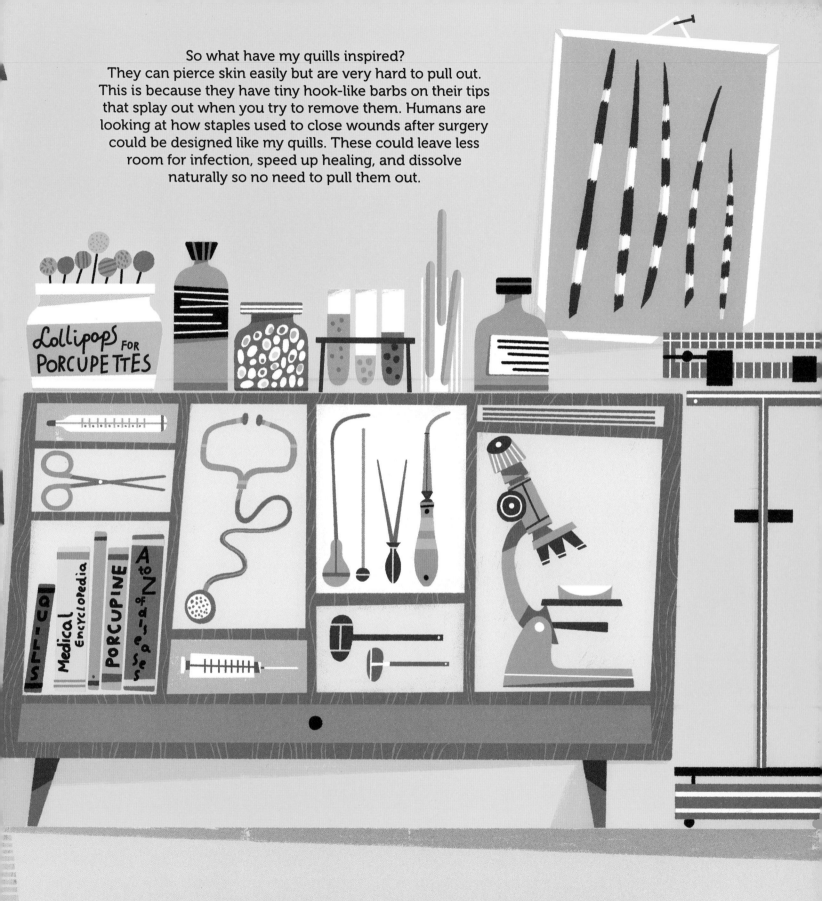

I am a natural medic. Not only are my quills inspiring cutting-edge medical
inventions, they are coated in a special greasy substance that is antiseptic.
This might be because I am pretty clumsy and can easily
spike myself when falling off a tree.

··· Slug ···
GOOEY SLIME

Slime is my world and I am covered in it from eyeball to tip. A life of slime isn't for everyone but it keeps me moving around on my big muscular body or "foot." I have two tentacles to feel my way around and two tiny eyes on long stalks that can stretch and wiggle. Unlike snails I don't have a fancy shell but can squeeze into the tiniest gaps. I don't have a bad bone in my body, in fact no bones at all!

GLUE

Glue

My slime is both slippery and sticky and it helps me to avoid drying out. With slime, I can glide over dirt and leaves, glue myself to wet things, and even climb up rocks and walls.

X-RAY

NO BONES

GLORIOUS SLIME

GOOES AND GLUES

GARDEN Veggies

Stick AND Slide

My sticky slime is the inspiration for a new kind of strong and stretchy glue that could one day be used to stick together bleeding cuts or wounds inside the human body. **It would be eco-friendly, just like my slime.**

GLUE

··· Mosquito ···
BLOOD—SUCKING NEEDLE

Us mosquitoes have a bad reputation and it is not surprising really. We usually sip the nectar and sap of plants, but when we lay eggs, we must drink fresh blood. Although most of us are harmless, some cause big problems by spreading diseases in hot tropical countries.

BLOOD TYPES

the ART OF stealth

How To Be INVISIBLE

DARTS

No one likes to be pricked with a needle. But our unique technique is inspiring humans to develop a surgical needle that could numb the skin and draw blood or inject medicine without pain. By taking a closer look at our super-efficient needle, they've worked out that its jagged edge, and the way that it vibrates when entering the skin, make it less painful and quite effortless.

The key to our finding a tasty drink of blood? Stealth. First, we land silently on our target and pierce their skin with our long needle-like mouth, or proboscis. We then inject spit to numb the skin so the host doesn't feel a thing. Our clever spit also stops the blood from clotting so the drink keeps flowing! Apart from the itchy red bump we leave behind as a calling card, you'd hardly know we had been. Then we fly off and find the perfect place to lay our eggs, usually a lake, pond, or puddle.

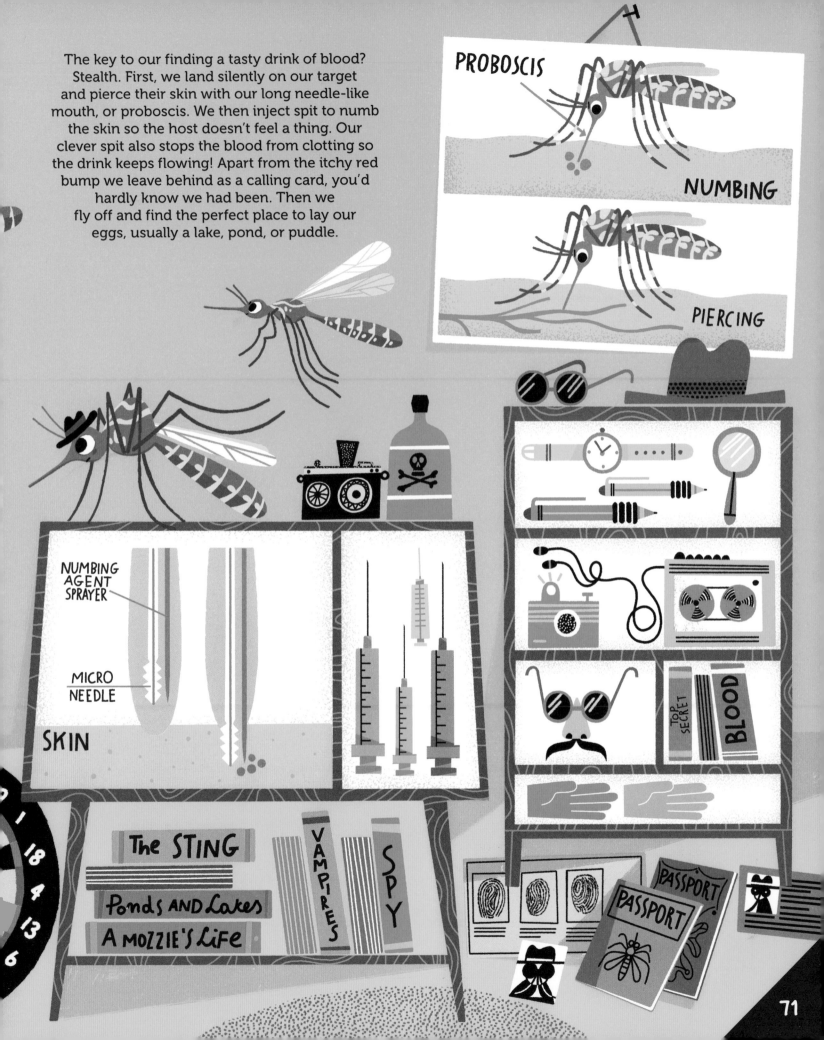

PROBOSCIS

NUMBING

PIERCING

NUMBING AGENT SPRAYER

MICRO NEEDLE

SKIN

The STING

Ponds AND Lakes

A MOZZIE'S LiFE

VAMPIRES

SPY

TOP SECRET

BLOOD

PASSPORT

PASSPORT

··· Dog and burrs ···
A STICKY SITUATION

Sure, people say I'm humans' best friend. But my best buddy when it comes to brilliant inventions would have to be this tall, prickly plant, the burdock. Together, we concocted the world's stickiest invention, Velcro.

One fine day in 1948, after a walk in the woods, my two-legged friend George de Mestral noticed that my fur and even his woolly socks were covered with sticky burrs that hold the small seeds of burdock plants. He took a closer look under a microscope and discovered hundreds of tiny hooks that can attach themselves to hairy fur like mine or loops of fabric. These allow the seeds to hitch a ride on passing animals and spread far away.

The sticky burrs gave George a great idea for a reusable hook-and-loop fastener. He designed a new way to join things together with two strips of fabric—one with tiny hooks like the burrs and one with tiny loops. The hooks and loops stick when they are pressed together and separate when pulled apart. The rest is history.

His invention hooked the world and soon replaced buttons, laces, zippers, and snaps. Think of all the things you have that stick with Velcro, from shoes and clothes to sports equipment, bags, wallets, toys, and watch straps! It's also used in automobiles, aircraft, and even on astronauts' spacesuits, as well as all the bits and bobs that can float away in the zero gravity space station. All this because George decided to take me on a walk through the woods!

ANIMAL INNOVATION LAB

Welcome to our innovation lab where we're constantly trialing and testing what works best in nature and have been doing for millions of years! Could our smart designs inspire the next big idea?

Sloth
HANGING ON

I spend most of my life hanging upside down from a tree. Could my knack for hanging on help build better suspension bridges or other hanging things?

Hippopotamus
ECO-FRIENDLY SUNSCREEN

I can stand in the scorching sun all day long without getting sunburned, as I produce a special sweat that blocks the sun. Could this inspire the invention of a waterproof and eco-friendly sun lotion, hopefully without the hippo smell?

HiPPO Sweat LOTiON

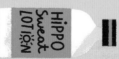

Wood frog
ANTIFREEZE

I can freeze myself solid in the cold winter and thaw out when it gets warmer. Could my chemical secret help to find better ways to freeze things? Or even create an eco-friendly antifreeze for automobiles, planes, and other machines?

Platypus
NAVIGATION

When I dive, I close my eyes, nose and ears and rely on my super-sensitive bill to navigate and find food in murky water. Could the special receptors on my bill help to improve navigation systems?

We are all part of the wonderful planet we live on. If humans take care of it, as we do, who knows what other amazing secrets we might let them in on! It's just a question of finding the right animal inventor for the job.

INDEX